Haddie Sue

and Seth Alan

I0370790

Haddie Sue
and the
Big Snowstorm

Written and Illustrated by Seth Roberts
Jesus is Real Series-Book 1

ISBN: 978-1-947998-00-1
Library of Congress Control Number: 2017914647

Copyright © 2017 by Seth Roberts
All rights reserved.

Published by Winter Evening Publishing
HC 62 Box 5095
Delta Junction, Alaska 99737
wintereveningpublishing.com

Scripture taken from the New King James Version. Copyright © 1982 by Thomas Nelson, Inc. Used by permission. All rights reserved.

This book or parts thereof may not be produced in any form, stored in a retrieval system or transmitted in any form by any means—electronic, mechanical, photocopy, recording, or otherwise—without prior written permission of the publisher, except as provided by United States of America copyright law.

Haddie Sue and the Big Snowstorm
is dedicated to my encouraging,
wonderful mother, Stephanie Roberts.

Winter Evening Publishing
Alaska

"My help comes from the Lord,
Who made heaven and earth."

Psalm 121:2

Look for all three of these on every picture!

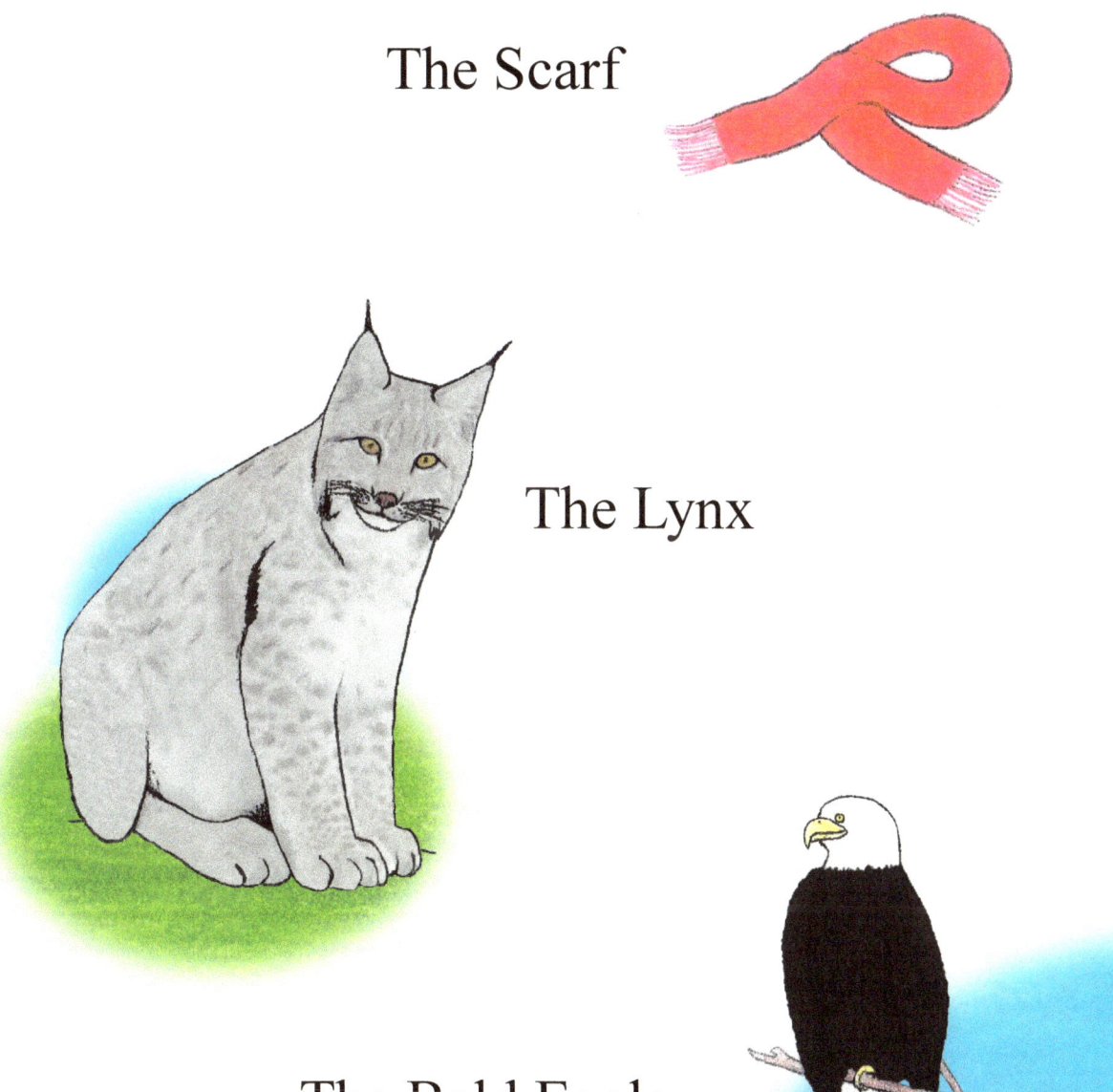

The Scarf

The Lynx

The Bald Eagle

Haddie Sue and her family had been shopping in the big city. They had bought a lot of groceries and were ready to drive to their home deep in the Alaskan woods four hours away. Haddie Sue, Mommy, Daddy, Brother, Doggy One, and Doggy Two jumped into their red van. Everyone was ready to go!

Their red van bounced and jiggled. Haddie Sue, Mommy, Daddy, Brother, Doggy One, Doggy Two, and all their groceries bounced and jiggled. They were driving up the steep mountainside to go home.

The air grew colder and snow started to fall. A storm began to blow as they went higher and higher up the steep, rocky mountain! All of a sudden, the red van began to chug, chug, rumble, and grumble!

Haddie Sue, Mommy, Daddy, Brother, Doggy One, and Doggy Two heard the strange noises and then they heard no noise! The engine had stopped chugging! The engine had stopped rumbling and grumbling! The red van had stopped working! They were stuck on the side of a high stormy mountain!

"Oh, no!" cried Haddie Sue. Everyone began to pray for another van to come that would take Haddie Sue, Mommy, Daddy, Brother, Doggy One, Doggy Two, and all their groceries home!

Haddie Sue saw Brother shivering and shaking. Brother saw Haddie Sue shivering and shaking. Haddie Sue looked at Brother's breath making clouds in the air. Brother looked at Haddie Sue's breath. It was getting cold—really cold!

What did Haddie Sue, Mommy, Daddy, Brother, Doggy One, and Doggy Two see? They saw two lights coming up the snowy mountain road toward their broken van that was sitting near the edge of a large cliff!

Haddie Sue prayed again! Everyone prayed again! The lights became brighter and brighter as the red van grew colder and colder. Was it a car? Was it a van? Was it a snowplow that would accidentally push them over the cliff?

It was a van! Two nice missionaries hopped out and let Haddie Sue, Mommy, Daddy, Brother, Doggy One, Doggy Two, and all their groceries go into the warm blue van.

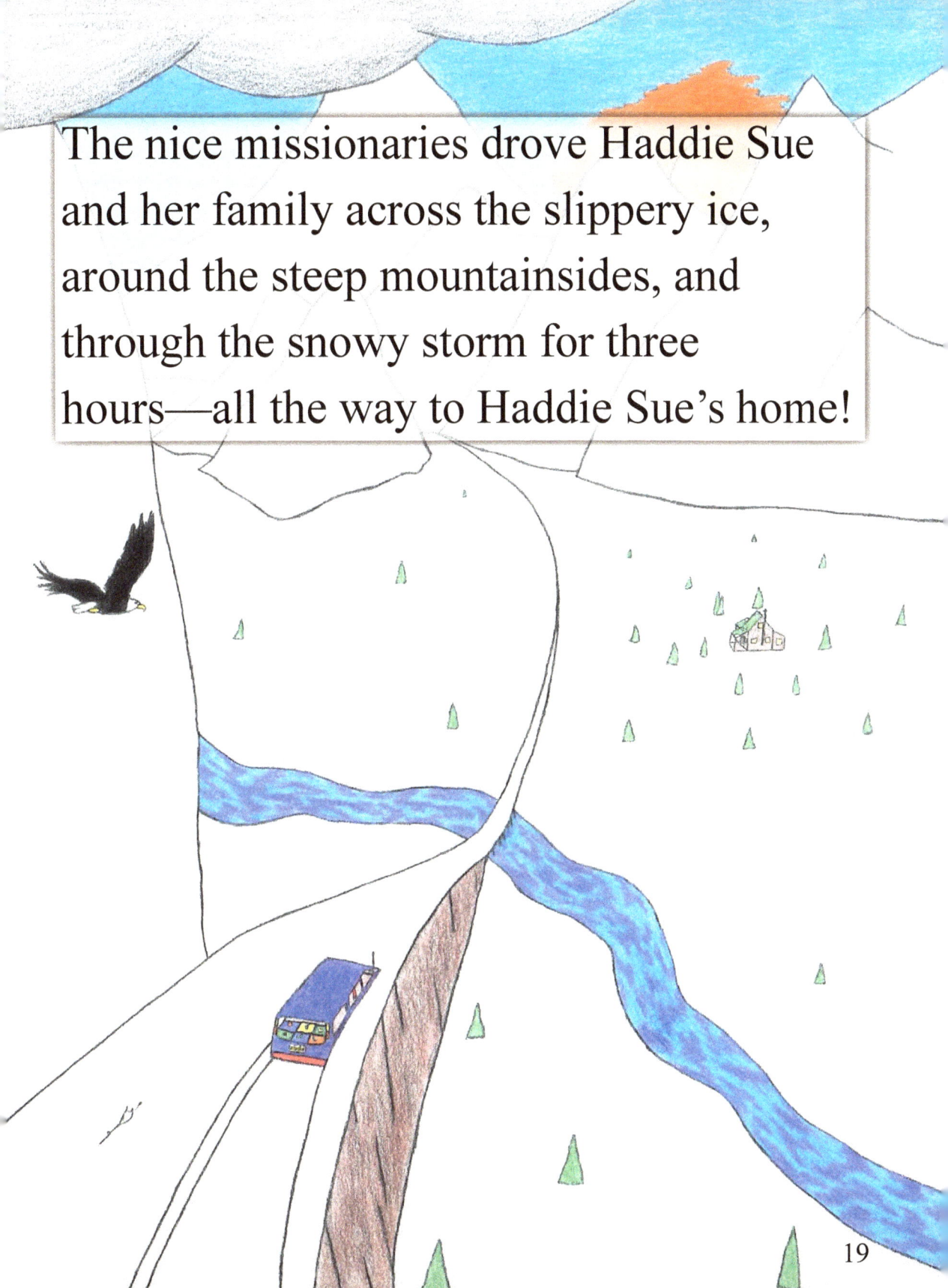

The nice missionaries drove Haddie Sue and her family across the slippery ice, around the steep mountainsides, and through the snowy storm for three hours—all the way to Haddie Sue's home!

Haddie Sue, Mommy, Daddy, Brother, Doggy One, Doggy Two, and all their groceries went inside their warm cabin deep in the Alaskan woods. They thanked Jesus for sending help and for bringing them safely home!

"For the Lord is good..."

Psalm 100:5

Watch for these books!

Haddie Sue and the Scary Noise

Enjoy the second adventure in the *Jesus is Real Series* as Haddie Sue and her family experience Jesus' protection!

Bear Country: The Adventures of a Young Man in Alaska

Older children and adults will enjoy the adventures of Seth Roberts as he and his family forge a life in remote Alaska and witness Jesus' protection, help, and guidance again and again!

www.ingramcontent.com/pod-product-compliance
Lightning Source LLC
Chambersburg PA
CBHW051251110526
44588CB00025B/2959